LIQUID ASSETS

"And remember, my dreams were dreamt privately and not on the National Health." 13.iii.75

LIQUID ASSETS

New Pocket Cartoons

by

OSBERT LANCASTER

JOHN MURRAY
1975

Osbert Lancaster's Other Works

PROGRESS AT PELVIS BAY
PILLAR TO POST
HOMES SWEET HOMES
A CARTOON HISTORY OF ARCHITECTURE
ALL DONE FROM MEMORY (Autobiography)
WITH AN EYE TO THE FUTURE (Autobiography)
SAILING TO BYZANTIUM
THE SARACEN'S HEAD
DRAYNEFLETE REVEALED
FACADES AND FACES
CLASSICAL LANDSCAPE WITH FIGURES
THE LITTLEHAMPTON BEQUEST

Pocket Cartoons

SIGNS OF THE TIMES 1939–1961
MEANINGFUL CONFRONTATIONS
PRIVATE VIEWS
THEATRE IN THE FLAT

———————

Grateful acknowledgement is made to the Editor for kind permission to reprint the drawings which have appeared in the *Daily Express*.

———————

*Printed in Great Britain for John Murray,
Albemarle Street, London at The Pitman Press, Bath*
0 7195 3238 8

FOREWORD

Eager as I always am to strike a note of brisk optimism in these biennial surveys, the achievement, I find, grows no easier with the years, while the counting of our blessings becomes annually less time-consuming. However, an ingrained determination to look on the bright side encourages me to make the effort.

In the period under review outbreaks of bubonic plague in the Home Counties have been mercifully few; southern England has been relatively untroubled by earthquakes; if the *ci-devant* Lord Stansgate continued to flourish like the green bay tree so, mercifully, did Mr. Bernard Levin; and it is just possible that in our reduced circumstances large-scale modern architecture is likely to remain beyond our means. "For these and all His great mercies. . . ."

O.L.

June 1975

"Three little maids from school are we. Our bras are
stuffed with T.N.T." 6.vi.72

"Quick, quick, Miss Bulstrode! Cyril's committing
environmental pollution!" 9.vi.72

13.vi.72

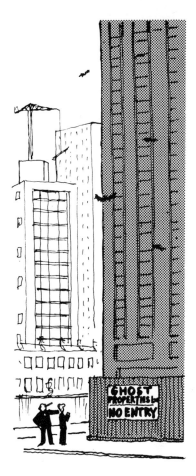

"One day, my boy, this will all be yours—and don't
you do anything silly like trying to let it!" 28.vi.72

"Let us never forget how privileged we are, sharing, as we do, the great cultural tradition of *la belle France*." 29.vi.72

"Heard the latest? The Borgias have been put on probation." 30.vi.72

"The object of the exercise, you understand, is to take his mind off the North Sea." 8.viii.72

"But, darling, I promise you I *never* called poor Louise a bastard—all I said was that I'd always understood she was the result of a regretted pregnancy." 10.viii.72

"Will Mrs Bracegirdle, winner of the Mothers'
Union Egg-and-Spoon Race, please come at once to
the Red Cross tent for a saliva test." 15.viii.72

"Why if it isn't God Almighty Superstar himself!"
16.viii.72

"Please, may I be a picket?" 30.viii.72

"I say, Daphne, isn't it *super* about the new Laureate?!" 11.x.72

"If you ask me, it's not the Russian winter that's going to fix Napoleon, but a good old English power-strike." 24.x.72

"Don't be a foolish virgin—stock up now!" 27.x.72

"Until that wretched Mrs Whitehouse piped up,
your dear grandfather had quite forgotten that he'd
got a ding-a-ling." 30.xi.72

"That'll make a nice change! Hitherto they've always taken jolly good care to look the other way."
10.i.73

"Why can't they be honest just for once and simply say 'Added Tax'?" 1.ii.73

"Dammit, Sir, when I was at school, the fifth Form
didn't *need* anyone from Gay Lib to come down and
tell them about homosexuality!" 9.ii.73

"Tell me, councillor, apart from returning contractors' hospitality what do you do with the rates?"
13.ii.73

"And another thing—you will kindly *not* refer to
great-aunt Edna as the Gross National Product."
24.ii.73

"I'm happy to tell you, gentlemen, that with a firm
lack of effort all round, our company should shortly
qualify for a very substantial hand-out of the tax-
payers' money." 21.iii.73

"Quite right, too! I myself have always made a point of cutting Mr Wilde." 30.iii.73

"*Nil desperandum,* boys! As a director of Cunard, Rolls-Royce, B.S.A. and a number of building societies I can assure you that there is always a silver lining if you know where to look for it." 6.iv.73

"I told you all along that Green Belts were just a lot
of eyewash!" 11.iv.73

"But Martin Bormann *must* be dead—if he were still alive he'd have had a job at the White House."
3.v.73

"We must be careful, dear, not to get so worked up about Watergate as to forget about Mr Poulson."
4.v.73

"Owing to the imminent collapse of the roof, Prof. Bauhaus' lecture on 'The Modern Movement in Architecture' has been transferred to the lacrosse ground." 26.vi.73

"Have you, by any chance, any soft porn?"
31.viii.73

EQUAL
OPPORTUNITIES
FOR BOTH
SEXES

18.ix.73

"It may say it's budgie food, Judson, but these
Fenians stick at nothing—open it in the servants'
hall!" 21.ix.73

"—And now for the good news!" 17.x.73

"Ever since they started drilling for oil in the glen,
the Laird's been a changed man." 19.x.73

"But surely the White House must still have *some* carpets left which they can brush things under?"
23.x.73

"How comes it that the Americans, with all their experience, always assassinate the wrong Presidents?" 30.x.73

"Tapes?! What tapes?" 2.xi.73

"More disasters! Boots have annexed Harrods and the United Nations haven't lifted a finger." 8.xi.73

"Sure an' why would Dr Kissinger not be coming to Dublin?!" 9.xi.73

"Of course if Lord Eccles gets what he thinks he's going to get by charging us to see our own property, it may almost foot the fuel bill for one Concorde test flight halfway across the Atlantic." 20.xi.73

"Cheer up, darling! There'll be no fall in the standard of living —it's just that we're all going to be a good bit worse off than we expected." 7.xii.73

"Some of us have been living in a State of Emergency, on and off, ever since we left the womb!"
13.xii.73

"From now on, man, we're working a one-tit week
for the duration of the emergency!" 11.i.74

"Food subsidies, pensions, social services all very
well—but if there's another penny for Maplin, Concorde, the Channel Tunnel or any more goddam
motorways I'll be right out there manning the
barricades" 26.iii.74

"To avoid disappointment I think I should warn you that dear Freda's martinis are definitely post-Budget." 4.iv.74

"By the way, I take it that you've no rooted objection to blue blood?" 9.iv.74

"Of course you can't go on wearing it—it's got more holes than an Irish jail." 17.iv.74

"What have I done with my life? I've never had any illegitimate children—I've never changed sex—I've never been offered a penny by Poulson!" 26.iv.74

"What's the latest from Watergate-on-Tyne?"
2.v.74

"Let us say, kind sir, that I have, just for the moment, a liquidity problem . . . .". 7.v.74

"And how many pedestrians' lives are compulsory
seat-belts expected to save?" 5.vi.74

"Feelthy tapes." 13.vi.74

"By the way, whatever happened to all that lovely nuclear power which was going to make coal quite unnecessary?" 19.vi.74

"Cheer up, Sir Ethelred! Always remember that things will have to get a lot worse before they get worse still." 21.vi.74

"Stand by for a couple of lepers and a nasty case of anthrax coming across from the private sector."
5.vii.74

"Personally, I'm in rather a tricky position—while my liver remains on the National Health, my prostate has passed into private hands." 16.vii.74

"I'm very much afraid that, right now, your dear father is busily engaged blowing his threshold in the bar at White's." 31.vii.74

"Father, I cannot tell a lie—besides, you've got the tapes." 7.viii.74

"Tell me, Lionel—your French is better than mine—what exactly is a *coup d'etat*?" 16.viii.74

"Don't get alarmed, Daddy darling, there's no question of wedding bells—it's just a social contract."
5.ix.74

"All one can safely say is that it won't be very long
before whichever lot gets in we'll be wishing to God
it hadn't." 10.x.74

"Has the bidding started yet?" 19.xi.74

"I wonder whether Mr Jenkins has ever checked up
on 'draconian'?" 27.xi.74

28.xi.74

"Too late!" 6.xii.74

10.xii.74

"Hither, page, and stand by me. Make a note, he's
self-employed!" 11.xii.74

"Just a moment, Santa Claus!" 24.xii.74

" . . . our flying time to London will be approximately one hour and thirty minutes, and we hope you enjoy your flight. Thank you!" 9.i.75

"D'ye remember tellin' me some years ago that ye thought that the internal combustion engine was here to stay? Well, now I'm not so sure ye were right." 10.i.75

"Don't quote me on this, dear, but I'm given to understand that Mrs Thatcher is not quite a gentleman!" 5.ii.75

" . . . and may I take this opportunity of reminding you, Postlethwaite, that we do *not* refer to the head-master as 'that silly old one-person child'." 7.ii.75

"I'm told that the trouble with Willie Hamilton is that he was once badly frightened by a corgi in his pram." 13.ii.75

"I think I should let you know, Filebrace, that I have decided to change my image." 20.ii.75

"You see, the great advantage of a referendum is that all expenses are chargeable to the tax-payer and there's no risk of anyone losing their seat." 27.ii.75

"And this, Sir Christopher, is Mrs. Rajagojollibami,
an enthusiastic European." 6.iii.75

"Comrades, our object is achieved—we've been invited to appear on World in Action!" 19.iii.75